time for a
Spiritual
Checkup

Gloria
Copeland

Time for a Spiritual Checkup

ISBN 978-1-60463-297-2   30-0576
20 19 18 17 16 15   6 5 4 3 2 1

© 2015 Gloria Copeland

Kenneth Copeland Publications
Fort Worth, TX 76192-0001

For more information about Kenneth Copeland Ministries, visit kcm.org or call 1-800-600-7395 (U.S. only) or +1-817-852-6000.

66 Examine and test and evaluate
your own selves to see whether
you are holding to your faith and
showing the proper fruits of it. 99

2 Corinthians 13:5
The Amplified Bible

table of Contents

Be Practical:
It's the Wise Thing to Do

Be Practical:
It's the Wise Thing to Do

Getting regular checkups is a good idea. Ken and I make a habit of it. Even though we're extremely healthy, full of energy and feeling good, we go to the doctor for routine exams because it's a wise thing to do. It helps us make sure that physically, we're staying on track.

Spiritually, we follow much the same practice. Even when everything in our lives is going fine, we check up on our faith regularly. We don't wait until some major problem arises and then rush around trying to find our Bibles to solve it. We spend time in the Word daily and routinely examine ourselves in light of it to make sure we're walking by faith in every area of our lives.

It's a practice I highly recommend. In fact, I'd go so far as to say it's essential for all believers who want to stay on track with what God has planned for them. I know from my own experience, God's Word is intensely practical for everyday life.

I've learned that God and His Word must have the preeminence in our lives. We shouldn't put anything—not career, ambitions, family or anything else—above God. When we put Him first, everything else will line up and be successful.

And, maintaining the best life He has for us requires these regular life examinations. We must examine our hearts and actions and find out if we're leaving any doors open to anything that would trip us up.

That's not just my opinion. Second Corinthians 13:5 confirms it. It says to all of us:

> Examine and test and evaluate your own selves to see whether you are holding to your faith and showing the proper fruits of it *(The Amplified Bible)*.

Examine Yourself

Notice, according to that verse, it's *ourselves* we must examine. We're the ones who need to be checked up on, not God. We don't have to evaluate Him to see if He's getting things right in answering our prayers, because He never misses it. If we've been asking Him for something and it seems like we're not getting anywhere, or if we aren't seeing His promises manifest in our lives, *He isn't the problem!*

The problem is on our end.

"Well, I don't know about that," someone might say. "I think I'd be doing fine if the people in my church were just more supportive. They aren't praying for me and standing with me like they should. So in my case, they're the problem."

No, they're not. If they were, the Bible would tell you to examine *their* faith. But it doesn't. It tells us to evaluate *ourselves*.

First John 5:4 says, "This is the victory that overcometh the world, even *our* faith." So when it comes to living in victory, our own faith—not someone else's—is the issue. Other people can't do our believing for us. Although at times we can and should help each other, ultimately our faith is our own responsibility. We're the ones who must get it going and working the right way. And, that requires that we expend some effort. It requires attention to the things of God, and the application of diligence, discipline and determination.

Don't Be a Wimp

The faith life is not for wimps. It's not for lazy people who just want to do what's easy on their flesh and don't want to nourish themselves with the Word. Nor is it for quitters who will just lie down and let life run all over them.

No, faith is for the strong of heart and the determined who will take the Word of God and act on it, regardless of the circumstances!

Faith is for the courageous. It's for the Joshuas who will stay in the Word day and night—meditate in it, talk it and do it. It's for the ones who desire to have good success in everything the Lord has called them to do (Joshua 1:8).

One of the marvelous things about faith in God's Word is that if you happen to be a "wimp" when you start out building or rebuilding your faith, if you'll begin to put the Word before your eyes and in your ears, get it into your heart, and then speak it out of your mouth, you'll be transformed. With every step of faith in God's Word, you become one of the strong ones!

That's what happened to Peter. When a big challenge came, he acted like a wimp. He denied three times the One he'd seen raise the dead, feed the multitudes and make the way for him to walk on water. (See Matthew 26; Luke 22.) In the garden of Gethsemane, Jesus warned him and the other disciples to watch and pray so they wouldn't fall into temptation. But he gave in to his flesh and fell asleep. When Jesus was arrested, he ran.

But, not too many days later, this fearful disciple who ran when the pressure was on, received the Baptism in the Holy Spirit and became a faith champion. He remembered the words he'd heard from Jesus and went on to preach a message on the day of Pentecost that got 3,000 souls saved (Acts 2:14-41)!

Faith in the Word he'd heard and the power of the Holy Spirit in Peter gave him the courage to become a champion. With every step of faith, the Word of God in *your* heart and the power of the Holy Spirit in *you*, like Peter, you too can be a champion!

Questions for Reflection

1. When was the last time you felt the need for a spiritual check-up? What were the circumstances? What did you learn about your spiritual health?

_____

_____

_____

2. When did you realize you alone are the one responsible for your faith and not anyone else? How has your life been different since that time?

_____

_____

_____

3. Think about times when you have been strengthened in your spirit by the Word. Can you think of a time when you knew you went from being a wimp to being strong?

_____

_____

_____

Notes

_____

_____

_____

_____

_____

_____

_____

_____

_____

_____

_____

_____

_____

_____

_____

_____

_____

_____

_____

_____

_____

_____

_____

_____

Be Proactive:
Have Faith in God

2

Be Proactive:
Have Faith in God

Faith in the Word of God is the strength of believers who will operate according to what Jesus taught in Mark 11:22-24 where He said to His disciples:

> Have faith in God. For verily I say unto you, That whosoever shall say unto this mountain, Be thou removed, and be thou cast into the sea; and shall not doubt in his heart, but shall believe that those things which he saith shall come to pass; he shall have whatsoever he saith. Therefore I say unto you, What things soever ye desire, when ye pray, believe that ye receive them, and ye shall have them.

When it comes to living by faith, these verses are the big guns. Ken and I can testify to that! We've depended on and lived them for more than 48 years. Time and again, they've helped us do, supernaturally, what we could never have done on our own.

So, let's use these verses to take a faith checkup right now.

The first thing they tell us is to "have faith in God." What, exactly, does that mean?

It's believing what you see in the Word regardless of what's happening in the natural realm. It's believing, even when you have symptoms of sickness in your body, that by Jesus' stripes "ye were healed" (1 Peter 2:24). It's believing, even when your stack of bills looks bigger than your bank account, that "God shall supply *all* your need according to his riches in glory by Christ Jesus" (Philippians 4:19).

How do you get that kind of faith? Actually, it's simple. According to Romans 10:17, it comes "by hearing, and hearing by the word of God."

Hear the Word

Take advantage of every opportunity to hear the Word. If you want to go from being a spiritual wimp to a spiritual champion, listen to anointed preachers and teachers. God has created technology that allows His Word to go out across the earth and be in our homes, our cars, our workplaces and wherever we happen to be, 24 hours every day. We can tune in to TV, radio, Internet, start up a CD or download at our convenience and readily receive the faith the Word provides. And, of course, we must get into a church that teaches what the Bible says about things.

You can believe God for anything you want that's in accordance with His Word! It doesn't matter how big or how impossible it might seem. Mark 10:27 says, "With God all things are possible." And, Mark 9:23 says, "All things are possible to him that believeth." With faith, you can have anything God has promised.

At one time, Ken and I were in what looked like an impossible situation to us. The ministry was millions of dollars in debt through television bills. The bills had multiplied by thousands and thousands of dollars every month. It just added up, and we weren't able to get ahead of it in the natural.

We were tempted to worry and, at one point, Ken even thought about selling ministry land to pay the bill.

But, what did we do instead? We believed God. We didn't run off and borrow any money. We used our faith and we *took* our deliverance, just as I've talked about. We believed that extra in. And that's what you can do. But you can't do it without giving God time. Spend time with Him and get in the Word. Just knowing what the Word says won't work because when you need a million dollars, you've been given a few weeks to live or you're facing some other impossible situation, your faith won't be able to take hold when you need it.

So what do you do? You get on the Word, and you stay there. You don't relent. Every day, you go over your scriptures and say, "I believe I receive it."

Isaiah 26:3 says, "Thou wilt keep him in perfect peace, whose mind is stayed on thee: because he trusteth in thee." *Perfect peace* means "everything right, everything blessed, everything done." *Stayed* means "sustained, supported." God's Word ministers to us, down in the deepest part of our hearts, just what we need, right when we need it, sustaining and supporting us.

Then, when that Word is rooted in us, faith has taken hold and goes off in our hearts—maybe we're sitting in a service, or reading the Bible by ourselves—all of a sudden, that impossible mountain staring us in the face looks easy to blow out of the way. That's when the mountain doesn't have a chance! But, it all starts in the heart. Once we get the image of victory from God's Word in our hearts and let it come out of our mouths, it's as good as done.

How do we get that kind of faith and image of victory in our hearts? By hearing the supernatural Word of God that's quick and alive and full of power. It's able to give you what you need, at that moment.

As you look at Mark 11:22-23, you learn that the key is your heart and your mouth.

Your very life depends on being full of God's Word. At the moment a crisis or challenge comes, if your heart is not full of what God says in His Word, you won't be able to speak His way. God's way, His Word, is the way of deliverance. He is the God of salvation and *deliverance.*

So you have to put God's ways, His thoughts, in your heart. That way, His words come out of your mouth when you need them.

God's Word is alive, active and operative. It's energizing and supernatural. He sends it out of His mouth, full of faith, to you—to your
heart. Those words from His mouth are supernatural Word seeds
He has sown. They are in His Book, and we can take out as much
as we want, anytime we want it.

Even though He spoke those words thousands of years ago,
they're still alive, active and full of power. They'll go down into
the very innermost parts of your being and become a sifter and
a discerner of the thoughts and the intents of your heart. Those
seeds will go into your heart and produce a crop.

God sows the Word out of His mouth that contains faith, and if
you've ever noticed, whatever He says always comes to pass. That's
why the Bible says, "With God all things are possible" (Mark 10:27).

God operates in a higher way than man does. What's impossible
to man is not impossible to God. He wants you to be that way, too.
He's given you faith words to put down into your heart that are
to come out of your mouth in the same way they come out of His
mouth (Romans 4:17).

This is the way you live in total victory right here in this crazy
world. You don't have to wait until you get to heaven. When
God's Word comes out of your mouth in faith, it produces a powerful crop that changes anything you can see.

Isaiah 55:11 says, "So shall my word be that goeth forth out of my
mouth: it shall not return unto me void, but it shall accomplish

that which I please, and it shall prosper in the thing whereto I sent it." *The Amplified Bible* says, "It shall not return to Me void [without producing any effect, useless]."

This says to us that God's words prosper when they come out of our mouths in faith, and bring forth the very specific things they were sent to do. If they're words about healing, they'll produce healing. Words about financial abundance will bring forth abundance. God's Word never fails.

It's a simple process: God's words come out of His mouth. You take them out of His Word, the Bible, and put them down into your heart. Then, you speak them out of *your* mouth back to Him. And, when those words go back to Him filled with faith, they produce the thing they were sent to accomplish. They produce the impossible.

For example, when the words for prosperity came into Ken's and my life, and we put them down into our hearts in abundance, they began to come out of our mouths. When they returned back to God in faith, our impossible financial situation began to turn around. Those words brought abundance from God. They will do the same for you. They'll work for whomever puts them to work.

The Word changes circumstances you could never change on your own. To God, all things are possible.

I don't care if you're believing to pay the rent and buy groceries, like we did when we started out. It works the same way if you're facing a $5 million television bill, or if your body is full of cancer and the doctors have given you no hope. God's Word will turn *any* situation around!

The word of faith says, "The word is nigh thee, even in thy mouth and in thy heart" (Romans 10:8). So if you need to make changes in your life, do a spiritual checkup. Find out what you need to do to get the Word down into your heart so it can come out of your mouth in faith and turn *your* situation around.

Then, look back at Mark 11:22-23 and purpose to change what you say. I don't care if people make fun of you. Whose life is it anyway? Those people are never around when you need them. God's Word works!

God's always around. Hebrews 13:5 says He will never leave us nor forsake us. This is the way He works. It's faith in His Word that causes things to change in this earth realm.

Let's continue with our faith checkup. Jesus said in Mark 11:22, "Have faith in God." And then in verse 23, "For verily I say unto you, That whosoever shall say unto this mountain, Be thou removed, and be thou cast into the sea; and shall not doubt in his heart...." There's the mouth and heart. "But shall believe that those things which he saith shall come to pass; he shall have whatsoever *he saith.*"

That scripture is enough to blow any problems out of your life. That mountain represents whatever impossible thing is standing before you. Say to it, "Be removed, be gone from me!" When you refuse to doubt in your heart because it's so full of God's Word that when you open your mouth, faith comes rushing out, then that mountain will be blasted out of the way. It's not a mental process. We're not talking about not doubting in your mind, we're talking about not doubting in your *heart*.

If you're doing your checkup and you know you're still doubting in your heart, there's only one way to change what your heart believes. And that's to put the Word in it until faith comes. Maybe you had enough Word in your heart 10 years ago to overcome a financial situation. But, we're talking about faith now. Hebrews 11:1 says, *"Now* faith is the substance of things hoped for."

You can't believe in your heart just because you make a decision to do it. A mental decision won't move the mountain. Only faith coming from a heart filled with God's Word will do the job: Remember, Mark 11:23 says, "...and *shall not doubt in his heart,* but shall believe those things which he saith shall come to pass; he shall have whatsoever he saith" (Mark 11:23).

When you've done your homework and you know your heart is full of the Word for your situation, it's time to have confidence that when you speak to the mountain it will remove. Notice, verse 23 also says, "...but shall believe that those things which *he saith* shall come to pass; *he shall have whatsoever he saith."*

You know your own heart. If your believing level is not at the place where you can get hold of your words in faith and speak to the mountain, it just means you have some work to do to get enough Word in your heart to deal with that situation.

So, get busy and get some more Word. You can do it! If you have to, listen to faith messages hour after hour, until the Word in you gets bigger than the problem you're staring at.

You won't get it by just sitting around waiting for it to fall on you like ripe cherries off a tree. You have to be proactive about it. If you have a need or desire for something, search the Word and find out what God says about it.

I've been a student of the Word for a long time, and I encourage you to do the same thing. Sit down with your Bible every day and read it. A daily meeting with just you, God and His Word is the most important time of your day. And when you come across something in the Word you'd like to know more about, or there's something He prompts you to search out, get in there and dig deeper. Make good use of all the study helps and tools available. Use a concordance, a dictionary, and a good commentary—many of which are available online. Most importantly, use your time to learn more about God and His Word. Every time you sit down to receive from His Word, God will never fail to reveal His goodness to you. He will always increase your faith in Him!

Do Some Homework

Personally, I like to put together lists of scriptural promises for all different areas of my life. I have lists of verses about healing, and about family matters. I also have a list of prosperity promises. Those lists help me a lot.

If you haven't already done it, I'd encourage you to put your own lists together. That way, when you face a challenge and the pressure is on, you'll know right where to go. If the flu starts going around at the office, you can get out your healing scriptures list and immediately shore up your faith.

When your bank account takes a hit from some unexpected need, you can run to your list of prosperity scriptures and strengthen your faith in God's Word that He's your provider. You can speak His Word that He meets all your needs and brings wealth to you!

Even better, you can go over those lists all the time. You can stay strong and ready for anything the devil tries to throw at you by feeding your spirit every day on God's promises. If things don't seem to be moving along in some area like you think they should, double up on your intake of the Word in that area and get rid of any doubt that tries to creep into your heart. Remember, verse 23 says, "Whosoever...shall not doubt in his *heart,* but shall believe that those things which he *saith* shall come to pass...." Your heart and your mouth are the keys.

The good life, the blessed life, the fun life, the effective life God desires for you comes from His Word. Use it like a daily dose of vitamins to keep you strong. Put the Word in your eyes and in your ears. Get it down into your heart. Say it out of your mouth. Do it when everything is going well with you, and especially when it seems like it's *not* going so well. You'll find your strong spirit will rise up in the face of any challenge that may come.

That's what Ken and I have been doing ever since we first started hearing about faith. As a result, we've become absolutely addicted to the Word of God. We became serious about the Word, and we're still serious about it. Many years have come and gone, and God has called us to do a lot of things—impossible things. He has given us faith projects that only He could accomplish. So we've simply believed Him, doing exactly what we've talked about here, and He has completed countless numbers of them through us.

We've learned from experience that whatever might come against us, we can come through it in victory by putting the Word into our hearts until it comes out of our mouths in faith back to God, and then *staying* in faith. Our answer to completing every task He has called us to do and overcoming every challenge we have faced, has been *His Word*.

Yes, we have had times when we got behind on bills, or something we were standing in faith for was slow in coming through. But we watched our words. Instead of saying at those times, "It's not working," we just doubled up on the Word of God deposited in our hearts, spoke it out of our mouths in faith, and kept moving forward. We are happy to report God's Word has never failed us!

So, whether it's a health challenge, lack in some area of your life or something going on with your children, faith in God and His Word works in *every* situation.

Questions for Reflection

1. Name the ways you spend time daily with God and in His Word. What kinds of audio technology or preaching do you regularly take advantage of?

_____

_____

_____

2. Have you developed your scripture list or do you have a resource that you use as your "go to" to help you recall particular scriptures in the face of challenges? (You'll find a great resource in the "Real Help" section of our kcm.org website to help you develop your scripture list.)

_____

_____

_____

3. Think about a challenge you faced or a faith project God called you to complete that looked impossible in the natural. How did you approach it, and what was the outcome?

_____

_____

_____

NOTES

Be Purposeful:
Speak Directly to the Mountain

Be Purposeful:
Speak Directly to the Mountain

O nce you have the lists of "go to" scriptures, use them! Use the scriptures and establish the faith in your heart so when you speak the Word, you have no doubt the mountain is coming down!

> Whosoever shall say unto this mountain, Be thou removed, and be thou cast into the sea; and shall not doubt in his heart, but shall believe that those things which he saith shall come to pass; he shall have whatsoever he saith (Mark 11:23).

The mountains in our lives take on many forms—health issues, financial matters, important decisions, relationship challenges—but the Word covers *every* form of *every* mountain that may show up.

Whatever mountain shows up, be purposeful and determined to bring it down. Your list of scriptures will keep you focused on the kind of mountain you're facing. Is it a health issue—a sickness or injury? Find healing and wholeness scriptures and declare strength and wholeness in that part of your body. Tell that mountain to be removed, and speak the truth of God's Word about the situation.

Is it a financial issue? Go to your prosperity and debt-freedom scriptures. Maybe you need to make an important decision. Go to your wisdom, knowledge and understanding scriptures. Or, if it's a relationship issue, go to your love and forgiveness scriptures.

It's the same process for every mountain you may be facing. Speak to it to be removed or the situation to be changed according to what God says. Command it to line up with the Word, and the Word will back you up.

When you speak to the problem or the situation and tell it what to do, be specific. Have confidence in your command to the mountain based on what you know God has said. Use your list of scriptures!

Then believe your words—God's words you have spoken will come to pass. That's how faith operates.

═══ Keep the Mountain Down ═══

Once you have spoken to the mountain and told it to be removed, and you've declared the Word of God over it, don't let any other words come out of your mouth that would bring the mountain back on the scene. Anytime sickness attacks your life, don't call everyone and tell them you're sick. Don't talk to people about the problem, tell them how the Word is taking it out of your life.

If you are believing for debt freedom, you're going to have to talk to that mountain of debt staring you in the face. Build your faith with the Word and when faith rises up in your heart, command debt to be removed from your life. If you find yourself talking to someone about the mountain, then tell them how you've talked to it and what scriptures you've spoken over it to see it removed. Those scriptures coming from your mouth build faith—maybe in someone else's life, too.

And, regarding finances, Ken and I learned early on, when we were so deeply in debt, that the Word says, "Owe no man any thing, but to love one another" (Romans 13:8). We thought that meant we would never be able to do anything financially. So, we checked another translation. But it said, "Keep out of debt." We'd already made the commitment that whatever we saw in the Bible, that's what we'd do. But, we'd always lived on borrowed money. I mean, I married Kenneth Copeland and his notes. And they were always with us. It seemed like they grew supernaturally. Everything we did, we did on borrowed money.

We thought, *If we don't borrow money, we'll never be able to have the ministry that God wants us to have. We'll never even have a car to drive, much less a house to live in.* We didn't know anything about the laws of prosperity then. But, we were determined to act on God's Word, even when we couldn't see how the results were ever going to bless us.

The thing I wanted most in the world was a home, but whoever heard of paying cash for a home? We were living in a little, dumpy house near a river, furnished in early Goodwill. We had been borrowing money, and we didn't have anything. It just looked to me that if we said we weren't going to borrow any more money, we would never have anything in the material realm.

But, we obeyed God's Word anyway, and stuck to our decision not to borrow any more money and to stay out of debt. We set our faith and agreed to owe no man anything but to love him, even though we thought we were costing ourselves material blessings by doing that. God began to teach us how He operates. He doesn't borrow money, either! We began learning to do things His way.

We spoke the Word to the mountain and started believing to get out of debt. It took us 11 months. From the very first day we spoke our faith, things began to get better. We decided: "We're going to give our attention to the Word of God. We're going to put it first place in our lives. We're going to operate in what God says, regardless of the circumstances." It took a few months to get out of debt, but it had taken a few *years* to get there!

It may have taken years to get your life in the mess it's in today. If you'll put the Word first place and listen to God, He will help you get it straightened out. It might not happen before dark tonight, but it will happen if you'll stand fast on the Word of God.

Deciding to live without a mountain of debt is a life-changing act of faith in God! It's more than just "staying out of debt." This kind of faith life is totally dependent on trusting God to be your provider and standing firmly in faith on what He has promised in His Word.

═══ Develop Faith for Life ═══

God gives us life to live on purpose. Our main purpose is to plant ourselves firmly in His Word and live every day according to His will for us. Proverbs 4:20-23 tells us clearly that God's Word is our source of life:

> My son, give attention to my words; incline your ear to my sayings. Do not let them depart from your eyes; keep them in the midst of your heart; for they are life to those who find them, and health to all their flesh. Keep your heart with all diligence, for out of it spring the issues of life *(New King James Version)*.

How we think, the decisions we make and what we do, determine the quality of our lives. The most important thing is that we're connected to God, and we believe we receive all the good things life in Him has to offer. We get connected to Him and His plan for our lives through His Word.

As we develop a working knowledge of the Scriptures about every area of our lives, we'll begin to truly live life God's way. Not only that, but we'll begin to gain understanding of His character, how He operates in the world and in our individual lives.

When we apply His wisdom to our everyday circumstances, taking a firm stand of faith on the Word about everything, He will guide us, step by step, into the life He intended for us.

As you can see, this life of faith is for the determined. So, set your heart every day to pay attention to God's Word and to spend time with Him. Faith will flow from a heart full of the Word to speak to any mountain that would dare try to stand in your way. Those mountains will have no choice but to move!

1. When was the last time a mountain in your life seemed to loom large before you? Think about how you addressed it. Would you do anything differently now?

_____

_____

_____

2. Think about where you are financially. Has God specifically spoken to you about the issue of debt? How have you responded?

_____

_____

_____

3. How has your purposeful, personal attention to God's Word changed your life?

_____

_____

_____

NOTES

Be Persistent:
What You Pray and Say Is What You Take

Be Persistent:
What You Pray and Say Is What You Take

The next thing you want to examine in your faith checkup is what Jesus taught about receiving in Mark 11:24: "What things soever ye desire, when ye pray, believe that ye receive them, and ye shall have them." The word translated *receive* there literally means "take," so that verse is telling us we'll have what we take in prayer.

How do we *take* something when we pray? With the words of our mouths!

We say to the Lord after we've made our request: "Thank You, Heavenly Father, for giving me what I asked. I believe I receive it. According to Your Word, it's mine. I have it now, in Jesus' Name." We receive it *when we pray!*

A lot of believers neglect to do this. They pray for what they desire, all right, but then they walk out of the place of prayer without it. Say, for instance, they need healing. Instead of saying, "I take my healing now, Lord. I thank You that I'm healed!" they say just the opposite. As soon as they finish praying, they'll call a cousin on the telephone and say, "I'm so sick I can hardly see straight! I feel just terrible."

I know what you're probably wondering. *What am I supposed to say at times like that? If I pray for healing, and someone calls before it manifests and asks me how I'm doing, what am I supposed to say?*

Just say something like, "I believe I received my healing." You don't have to start listing all the symptoms you're experiencing. If the person persists in asking you about them, just start praising God and quoting the Word. Most likely, whomever you're talking to will either praise God along with you or find a quick way to end the conversation.

"But Gloria, is what I say really *that* important?"

According to Jesus, it is. He said, "Out of the abundance of the heart the mouth speaketh" (Matthew 12:34), and we shall have whatever we say (Mark 11:23). So, obviously our words are vital. They determine what happens in our lives.

Proverbs puts it this way:

- "Death and life are in the power of the tongue: and they that love it shall eat the fruit thereof" (Proverbs 18:21).
- "Thou art snared with the words of thy mouth, thou art taken with the words of thy mouth" (Proverbs 6:2).
- "Whoso keepeth his mouth and his tongue keepeth his soul from troubles" (Proverbs 21:23).

The bottom line is, if you don't want it, don't say it. If you do want it, take it, talk it and don't deviate. If you happen to get discouraged and mess up, then repent right away and get back on track. Be persistent! Keep believing and declaring God's Word, and you *will* receive your desires.

Take Your Healing

This is how you receive everything: healing, financial provision, children walking with the Lord and all the rest of God's BLESSINGS!

Once Ken and I got hold of the truth of God's Word about what we say, we focused on always talking in agreement with the Word about every situation.

To begin with, we learned that speaking the Word will keep the enemy's work out of our lives. So, we have lived in divine health, prosperity, relationships and THE BLESSING all these years. And, if something tries to attack us, we just double up on the Word in that area.

When symptoms of some illness try to latch on to us, we immediately go to one another and get into agreement in prayer and receive our healing right then, when we pray. We speak to the symptoms and tell them to be removed (as we would any mountain). Next, we begin to declare according to Isaiah 53:4-5: "Surely he [Jesus] hath borne our griefs, and carried our sorrows.... He was wounded for our transgressions, he was bruised for our iniquities:

the chastisement of our peace was upon him; and with his stripes we are healed."

We expect to be healed when we speak the truth of Psalm 103:2-3: "Bless the Lord, O my soul, and forget not all his benefits: who forgives all our iniquities; *who heals all our diseases.*"

We go to the Scriptures right away. You can see how important it is to have your list of scriptures right by your side so you can rebuke and resist every kind of attack immediately. Don't give the symptoms one moment to get a hold on your body or mind. Take your healing right then and there!

I will say that after all these years of living this kind of faith and being healed consistently by the Word, we don't have to go to the list so much. The Word has become so much a part of our being, planted deeply within our hearts and coming out of our mouths so often, these scriptures just come right to us every time we face a physical challenge.

Take Your Prosperity

This works the same for any financial needs we may have. Let's say I needed $10,000 right now.

First, Ken and I would come into agreement in prayer with our faith. We'd say, "Lord, we're asking You today for this $10,000 to complete this project. We tell this mountain of need to be removed. We touch it with our faith. We believe we receive $10,000 based on Your Word, and we take it, now!"

Then, we'd speak the truth of the scriptures we have used for all these years that promise He will meet our needs, like "My God liberally supplies all our needs according to His riches in glory by Christ Jesus." (See Philippians 4:19.)

Again, because we have gone to this scripture and others like it so often, they come right out of our hearts into our mouths when a need arises. We also speak them on a daily basis to ensure the prosperity the Lord has promised us.

Take Your Children

This living faith is how you receive your children coming into the kingdom of God. Claim their salvation according to the promises in the Word (Isaiah 54:13, 59:21). Then, thank the Lord for bringing them to Himself.

Speak to the mountain of deception in their lives and tell it to be removed. Say, "Satan, you're not getting my children! I break your power over them in Jesus' Name."

Although, for a while, you might not see any change in them, you just keep on saying, "I believe I receive. My children are coming into God's kingdom. I have it, and I'm not going to be moved by what they say or do to the contrary." You continue to believe God, and don't waver.

If your children are grown and off somewhere, involved in something crazy or with someone who's a bad influence, when you hear about it, you just hold your ground. You take authority over their lives and break the power of the devil over them. You say, "Satan, I bind you off my children. They're not yours. They're mine. I've committed them to God, and His will shall be done in their lives." Then, you keep right on standing in faith, believing God and not wavering until it comes to pass.

God will be faithful over your children. They may be on drugs. It may look like the worst situation. They may be in prison. But wherever they are, you stand your ground. You believe God for their deliverance and don't walk in fear. Your children may be 40 years old, but they're still your children. See the mercy of God hovering over them to deliver and to get laborers across their paths, until their lives can get straightened out.

Everything we desire from God comes to us by faith. If we don't put any faith out there believing for our children, then they're not going to have the supernatural help they need. Supernatural help from God in any area of life comes as we open the door to Him by believing and trusting in Him.

Take It All!

These are just a few of the things that matter most to us in life. The same faith process applies in every area. Whatever you have going on in your life, you can pray, believe and take all the desires of your heart by faith.

Do you have loved ones who are in harm's way? You can take your stand of faith on Psalm 91 and receive God's promised protection for them wherever they are.

Do you have a broken relationship that needs to be mended? You have the power to give and receive love and forgiveness according to God's Word and restore your relationship (Mark 11:25-26; Hebrews 3:13).

Do you have a situation at work, school or church causing problems for you and others? Your faith can bring peace to the situation and make all the difference.

You can be a blessing straight from God everywhere you go because you have faith in God to move mountains and to give you what you ask for in every situation. You can stand in faith for people and see change in their lives and yours.

Keep standing in faith, taking it all, and see how God comes through!

Questions for Reflection

1. Think, for a moment, of an example of how your words have affected your stand of faith.

_____

_____

_____

_____

2. Think about things you have prayed for. When did you receive the answers?

_____

_____

_____

_____

3. Going forward, how will you pray and speak about the issues that matter most to you?

_____

_____

_____

_____

NOTES

_____

_____

_____

_____

_____

_____

_____

_____

_____

_____

_____

_____

_____

_____

_____

_____

_____

_____

_____

_____

_____

_____

_____

Be Patient:
The Power Twins Always Win

Be Patient:
The Power Twins Always Win

Maybe you're thinking, *But, what if it takes a long time for what I believed I received in prayer to show up? What should I do while I wait?*

Obey James 1:4 and Hebrews 6:12: "Let patience have her perfect work…. [And] be not slothful, but followers of them who through faith and patience inherit the promises."

Ken recently described patience as "being steady on the Word of God and allowing THE BLESSING to work things out."

Patience is a powerful force. It holds you up when you're under pressure. It undergirds you so you don't let go of your faith in times of trial. Even when you're faced with contrary circumstances, patience doesn't quit. It keeps you believing God's Word and saying the right things.

Faith and patience working together are the power twins. So

when you're doing your faith checkup, it's important to examine your patience, too.

To be frank about it, I wish that weren't necessary. I wish everything we prayed for and took by faith would happen instantly. That would be great! But that's not generally what happens. Although some things we believe for might come quickly, other things will come more slowly.

This was true even in Jesus' life. Read in Mark 11 about His encounter with the fig tree and you'll see what I mean. When He cursed that tree by saying, "No man eat fruit of thee hereafter for ever" (verse 14), there was no immediate, visible change in the tree. It looked just the same right after He spoke to it as it had before.

But Jesus didn't let that bother Him. Instead, He exercised patience and kept believing what He said would come to pass. Sure enough, the next day when He and His disciples walked by the tree again, they saw it had "dried up from the roots" (verse 20).

What if Jesus hadn't exercised patience that day? What if He'd gotten discouraged because the fig tree didn't keel over the moment He spoke to it? What if He'd said, "Well, I guess My words didn't make any difference"?

What would have happened?

Nothing! If Jesus had pulled back on His faith, that fig tree would have just gone right on living.

The same principle holds true in our lives. If we don't let patience have her perfect work, and just pull back and give up when we don't see instant results, we'll cut off our supernatural receiving. We'll miss out on what we've been believing for.

═══ Pay Attention to Patience ═══

The most critical time when you're believing God for something is *after* you pray in faith, believing you receive (Mark 11:24), but *before* you see any evidence of the answer.

This is the crucial time when things are changing and being set in motion by your faith, though you can't *see* anything. It's the time when you're the most tempted to say, "Nothing is happening. I prayed and believed, but I don't have it. It looks like I never will. I guess I just don't have enough faith."

You may *want* to say that—but don't! The Bible says that every believer has received "the measure of faith" (Romans 12:3). When you're tempted to give up, what you need is something to strengthen and undergird your faith so it will continue working until the answer comes. What you need during this critical time is *patience.*

Patience is a fruit of the re-created human spirit that does not give in to circumstances or give up under trial. Patience doesn't quit believing. Patience supports faith to keep it stable and strong when circumstances shout, "It's impossible!"

Patience keeps you steadfast in your faith and steadfast in your confession. It keeps you from giving up.

The force of patience is so powerful, it cannot be overcome—if you exercise it. If you yield to it in a time of test or trial, it will come to your aid to help you stand. It will undergird your faith to keep you believing until the answer comes.

Let Faith and Patience Do Their Work

So, the next time you're tempted to say, "It's not working," yield to the force of patience instead. Faith and patience working together will make you a winner every time!

Faith with patience always wins the fight. So stay on the winning side. No matter how long it takes, keep believing until the fig tree withers, the symptoms leave your body, the money comes or the situation changes. Keep saying with confidence, "This is the victory that overcomes the world, even my faith!"

Stay steady on your faith, and let the Word work it out because no one in the whole world can stop your miracle but you. No one controls your heart and your mouth but you.

Put God's Word first place in your life and give yourself regular faith checkups. Use patience and faith to keep yourself in shape to stand strong in faith so you can take what God has promised. Then, hold on to it until it manifests in your life!

Questions
for Reflection

1. Name a time in the past when you were just on the verge of giving up, but God prompted you to keep up your faith and be patient. What was the outcome?

_____

_____

_____

_____

_____

_____

_____

2. What might have been the outcome had you given up?

_____

_____

_____

_____

_____

_____

_____

NOTES

Be a Powerhouse:
Being Blessed and Being a Blessing!

Be a Powerhouse:
Being Blessed and Being a Blessing!

Because you're born again, you are a powerhouse for God! You're filled with His Spirit and power that's ready to be released into the world—your world! Within you is the power to bring life instead of death into every situation you face. You hold the power to be blessed and to be a blessing.

The power in you is released as you stand strong in your faith in God and His Word. Give yourself regular spiritual checkups and become refreshed by the truth of God's Word. You'll discover the power God has placed in you to receive all He has promised and all He has in store for you to give out to other people.

His promises *will* come to pass. The Lord spoke to me back in the early days of our life in Him, while we were still learning how to stand strong. I was studying my Bible, taking notes, listening to Brother Kenneth E. Hagin, and I heard the Lord say: *In consistency lies the power.*

Ken and I began to see that we had to believe that our words carried authority and were coming to pass. We decided we were not going to speak words we didn't want to come to pass. We were learning that our words shape our future and that we were getting today exactly what we had said yesterday, last month and last year. What you say consistently is what you will have. Your future is stored up in your heart because out of the abundance of your heart, your mouth speaks. If you speak the Word of God, you're going to have a good future. The good man, out of the good treasure of his heart—the Word—brings forth good things. So when you put the Word of God into your heart as your treasure, you're going to bring good things to pass.

Now, give yourself a faith checkup in this area. Whatever is happening in your life today is the result of what you've said in the past. Begin to discipline your mouth to speak what you want to come to pass. Your faith doesn't just operate when you're on your knees praying. It operates all the time. Every word you utter has faith, or believing, behind it—whether good or bad. So, get your words in line with the good things you desire to come to pass in your life.

That's what Ken and I did. We began to believe and to discipline our mouths to speak what we wanted to come to pass—*consistently*.

If we didn't want sickness and disease, we didn't talk it. If we didn't want any more lack—and we'd had enough of that—we stopped talking it. *In consistency lies the power.* We began to consistently speak in line with the Word of God—not just in prayer, but all the time.

Sometimes it was tough because our flesh wanted to talk the problem. But, we disciplined our mouths to agree with what the Word said about it.

Back then, I became aware of the need to check up on myself regularly. So, I began to consistently pay attention to certain areas of my life. I began to examine myself by the Word.

I asked myself what I was listening to. Was I hearing the Word and building my faith so the words coming out of my mouth matched what we were believing for? Was I listening to the Spirit in my heart for His guidance and counsel? Was I allowing Him to teach me what He wanted me to know?

What was I putting before my eyes? Was it His Word? What was I giving my attention to? Was I staying focused on the Lord and His plan for my life?

What was I saying? Where and how was I spending my extra time? Was my faith receiving the blessings God had for me and producing the blessings for me to give to people He had placed in my life? Was I standing strong in faith?

Second Corinthians 13:5 (*The Amplified Bible*) says, "Examine and test and evaluate your own selves to see whether you are holding to your faith and showing the proper fruits of it."

Staying Strong, Always

Back then, it took a while, but now I take the time, often, to examine my life and see how strong I am. I don't put it off until I'm in the middle of some test or trial.

There will always be challenges of some sort throughout the days we're on this earth: health concerns, financial trouble, relationship challenges. They're inevitable. Jesus said, "In the world you will have tribulation." But He didn't stop there. He added, "But be of good cheer, I have overcome the world" (John 16:32-33, *New King James Version*).

Hearing those words from Jesus produces faith in us. And, we can make the same declaration because He has given us the same world-overcoming faith He has! We are born of God and our victory over every trial and tribulation is our faith in God and His Word (1 John 5:4).

God's answers for every test we face are in His Word. All we have to do is go to it, open it up, find the answer and take the few simple steps we have looked at to solve every problem. You can see, once again, just how important having that scripture list is for you to be consistently strong in faith.

Back to Basics

Since the beginning, God has intended for our lives to be lived by faith. Every decision we must make boils down to our faith in what God has said. Our spiritual and physical health depend on it. The main issue for all our decisions is whether or not we choose to believe His Word and take what He has stored up for us.

Think about it. From every morsel of food we put into our mouths, to how we obtain the things we need, to how we treat the people in our lives—it's up to us whether our choices result in life and blessing or death and cursing.

When you and I made the most important decision in our lives to receive Jesus as Savior and Lord, we truly opened the door to everything good God has for us. When we said, "Yes, I believe Jesus is the Son of God, and I receive Him as my Savior and Lord," the Spirit of God moved into our lives and we were empowered to begin living the life of faith. We were miraculously given the ability to hear directly from God in our hearts and to understand clearly what the Bible has to say about us and the issues in our lives. The Spirit of God moved inside our spirits to teach us God's wisdom concerning everything we need to know for a victorious life.

The choice is still up to us whether we'll take advantage of the answers and solutions the Holy Spirit wants to reveal to us in His Word and in our spirits, or just sit there and keep complaining and letting life get us down.

Choose the Blessed Life

The blessed life is a life lived by faith in God. It may be faced with challenges every day, but it will stand strong in faith above every one of them.

Faith makes it its business to know God's Word on every subject, or to find out what He has to say about it. God's Word is not silent on any issue in life.

We all deal with the same issues Adam and Eve dealt with. All of mankind's challenges started with them. And, the choice to respond in faith is still the same: Who will you listen to? Who will you obey?

God has never taken away mankind's ability to choose how we will handle the trials and tribulations that come against us. Even with all the power of the Holy Spirit we have received to tap in to His wisdom, knowledge and understanding, the questions come down to this: "Will I spend the time today to hear from God? Will I get my information from the Word or from the world? Will I take the time to receive His truth that will give me the blessed life?"

When you choose God's way, you'll have your answers right before your eyes and in your ears, so they're the first thing out of your mouth when challenges come. This isn't rocket science. But I'll tell you this: Approaching your life from this simple perspective of faith in God and His Word will determine how far and fast you'll go in life.

It's God's plan for you to succeed and to be living proof that anyone can live the blessed life Jesus came to give us. What will you choose?

Spiritual Health Exam

God has a great spiritual health plan for each of us. He's laid it out in His Word. Our most important role in His plan is to pay attention to what He says. Give attention to the Word with your ears, your eyes and your heart. As we keep ourselves consistently submitted to being examined by the Word and keep making the adjustments we need to keep on track, the Word will keep us headed in the right direction and bring God's plans for us to pass.

God intends for each day of our lives to be blessed. Remember what He said through the prophet Jeremiah to the children of Israel: "'For I know the plans I have for you,' says the Lord. 'They are plans for good and not for disaster, to give you a future and a hope'" (Jeremiah 29:11, *New Living Translation*). That's His No. 1 plan for *all* His children.

"Plans for good and not for disaster." God's big picture is that nothing in your life is a disaster and that nothing cuts off His plan for your good, hope-filled future!

So, stay spiritually checked up with God. Give the Holy Spirit who lives in you and guides you, something to work with. This is how God has directed me for more than 40 years of facing and overcoming the challenges in my life. I always give God the first part of my day. I read His Word, I pray in the spirit and I listen to Him. I pay attention.

Sometimes, He directs me to go about my daily business and be ready for whatever He brings my way. Other times, He'll direct me to step out and go somewhere special or call someone about something. I make a point to operate by faith in Him every day, and listen for His direction.

Always be open to God's direction. There may be something in your life that needs adjusting or maybe an outright change. Maybe an attitude needs to be changed or an activity needs to be reconsidered. Or, perhaps a perspective needs to be tweaked. When you approach your heavenly Father every day in faith, do it with an attitude that says, "God, I'm open to adjustment. Show me where I need to be tuned up and brought into alignment with Your Word."

Like everyone, I've had some major challenges in my life. But, praise God, because of these regular faith checkups, consistently paying attention and spending time with Him in the Word, I've kept myself prepared and have overcome *every* challenge. You can do the same.

Some of the challenges I have overcome have appeared and gone in a day. Some have just needed a small adjustment, and some have required a major overhaul! Some have taken weeks, months or years to be resolved. But the solutions have *always* come. They have come because Ken and I have made the effort to stay in the Word and in faith. We have kept our focus on God, given Him our attention and obeyed Him. We know that every kind of problem we will ever face will be solved, and every mountain we will ever face will come down. God is faithful. He has proven that to us, and we know of no other way to live.

= Strong Faith Works Without Fail =

Problems come and go. Trials rise and fall. But victory has become permanent for us because we stay in the Word of God and obey it. We have become strong in faith. Anyone can do it. There's no reason to stay under any circumstance. As Ken says, "There may be excuses, but there are no reasons." Faith works *every* time, without fail.

God is good, and He is always for us!

He has done everything required for us to overcome every challenge and obtain victory in every trial.

As I've said, His ultimate purpose is that we live blessed and live to bless others. It's all His idea!

Yes, we are all challenged in the major areas of life. Health and healing are part of the strong life of faith. God has the answer, and we can be whole and well.

Finances and provision are wrapped up in our faith in God. When we're challenged and tempted to turn to the world's information to have our needs met, we can turn to Him instead.

Thriving relationships are also part of our blessing. They may come under attack, but we can always win.

When we're armed with and rely on His Word every day, there's no reason to fear failure. We'll have the kind of faith that will stand strong and carry us through to victory.

So, get into the Word, study it, find its answers, and speak to your mountain. Believe you receive when you pray. If I can do it, you can, too!

Today, you can start building your never-failing, strong faith for the BLESSED life! Become the powerhouse of faith God has in His heart for you to be. Become the blessing He needs you to be to the world.

Take the time to give yourself a faith checkup. Find out how strong you are in your faith and determine if you need to change anything. And, most importantly, *have faith in God.* Open the Word, stay in it, hear it, speak it and do it.

Be blessed, and BE A BLESSING!

Questions for Reflection

1. Look at that last paragraph and think about how strong in faith you are today. Ask the Lord to show you.

_____

_____

_____

2. What adjustments, if any, is the Lord prompting you to make so you'll have strong faith?

_____

_____

_____

3. Write down the first steps you'll be taking to keep your faith strong in the days ahead.

_____

_____

_____

Remember, the Lord said, *In consistency lies the power.* Do these things every day and you'll be ready to enjoy the life God has promised!

NOTES

Prayer for Salvation and Baptism in the Holy Spirit

Heavenly Father, I come to You in the Name of Jesus. Your Word says, "Whosoever shall call on the name of the Lord shall be saved" (Acts 2:21). I am calling on You. I pray and ask Jesus to come into my heart and be Lord over my life according to Romans 10:9-10: "If thou shalt confess with thy mouth the Lord Jesus, and shalt believe in thine heart that God hath raised him from the dead, thou shalt be saved. For with the heart man believeth unto righteousness; and with the mouth confession is made unto salvation." I do that now. I confess that Jesus is Lord, and I believe in my heart that God raised Him from the dead.

I am now reborn! I am a Christian—a child of Almighty God! I am saved! You also said in Your Word, "If ye then, being evil, know how to give good gifts unto your children: HOW MUCH MORE shall your heavenly Father give the Holy Spirit to them that ask him?" (Luke 11:13). I'm also asking You to fill me with the Holy Spirit. Holy Spirit, rise up within me as I praise God. I fully expect to speak with other tongues as You give me the utterance (Acts 2:4). In Jesus' Name. Amen!

Begin to praise God for filling you with the Holy Spirit. Speak those words and syllables you receive—not in your own language, but the language given to you by the Holy Spirit. You have to use your own voice. God will not force you to speak. Don't be concerned with how it sounds. It is a heavenly language!

Continue with the blessing God has given you and pray in the spirit every day.

You are a born-again, Spirit-filled believer. You'll never be the same!

Find a good church that boldly preaches God's Word and obeys it. Become part of a church family who will love and care for you as you love and care for them.

We need to be connected to each other. It increases our strength in God. It's God's plan for us.

Make it a habit to watch the *Believer's Voice of Victory* television broadcast and become a doer of the Word, who is blessed in his doing (James 1:22-25).

About the Author

Gloria Copeland is a noted author and minister of the gospel whose teaching ministry is known throughout the world. Believers worldwide know her through Believers' Conventions, Victory Campaigns, magazine articles, teaching audios and videos, and the daily and Sunday *Believer's Voice of Victory* television broadcast, which she hosts with her husband, Kenneth Copeland. She is known for Healing School, which she began teaching and hosting in 1979 at KCM meetings. Gloria delivers the Word of God and the keys to victorious Christian living to millions of people every year.

Gloria is author of the New York Times best-seller, *God's Master Plan for Your Life* and *Live Long, Finish Strong,* as well as numerous other favorites, including *God's Will for You, Walk With God, God's Will Is Prosperity, Hidden Treasures* and *To Know Him.* She has also co-authored several books with her husband, including *Family Promises, Healing Promises* and the best-selling daily devotionals, *From Faith to Faith* and *Pursuit of His Presence.*

She holds an honorary doctorate from Oral Roberts University. In 1994, Gloria was voted Christian Woman of the Year, an honor conferred on women whose example demonstrates outstanding Christian leadership. Gloria is also the co-founder and vice president of Kenneth Copeland Ministries in Fort Worth, Texas.

Learn more about Kenneth Copeland Ministries by visiting our website at **kcm.org**

Materials to Help You Receive Your Healing
by Gloria Copeland

Books

* * And Jesus Healed Them All
* * God's Prescription for Divine Health
* * God's Will for Your Healing
* * Harvest of Health
* Words That Heal (gift book with CD enclosed)

Audio Resources

Be Made Whole—Live Long, Live Healthy
God Is a Good God
God Wants You Well
Healing Confessions (CD and minibook)
Healing School

DVD Resources

Be Made Whole—Live Long, Live Healthy
Know Him As Healer

*Available in Spanish

When The LORD first spoke to Kenneth and Gloria Copeland about starting the *Believer's Voice of Victory* magazine...

He said: *This is your seed. Give it to everyone who ever responds to your ministry, and don't ever allow anyone to pay for a subscription!*

For more than 40 years, it has been the joy of Kenneth Copeland Ministries to bring the good news to believers. Readers enjoy teaching from ministers who write from lives of living contact with God, and testimonies from believers experiencing victory through God's Word in their everyday lives.

Today, the *BVOV* magazine is mailed monthly, bringing encouragement and blessing to believers around the world. Many even use it as a ministry tool, passing it on to others who desire to know Jesus and grow in their faith!

Request your FREE subscription to the
***Believer's Voice of Victory* magazine today!**

Go to **freevictory.com** to subscribe online, or call us at
1-800-600-7395 (U.S. only) or **+1-817-852-6000**.

We're Here for You!®

Your growth in God's Word and your victory in Jesus are at the very center of our hearts. In every way God has equipped us, we will help you deal with the issues facing you, so you can be the **victorious overcomer** He has planned for you to be.

The mission of Kenneth Copeland Ministries is about all of us growing and going together. Our prayer is that you will take full advantage of all The LORD has given us to share with you.

Wherever you are in the world, you can watch the *Believer's Voice of Victory* broadcast on television (check your local listings), the Internet at kcm.org or on our digital Roku channel.

Our website, **kcm.org,** gives you access to every resource we've developed for your victory. And, you can find contact information for our international offices in Africa, Asia, Australia, Canada, Europe, Ukraine and our headquarters in the United States.

Each office is staffed with devoted men and women, ready to serve and pray with you. You can contact the worldwide office nearest you for assistance, and you can call us for prayer at our U.S. number, 1-817-852-6000, 24 hours every day!

We encourage you to connect with us often and let us be part of your everyday walk of faith!

Jesus Is LORD!

Kenneth & Gloria Copeland

Kenneth and Gloria Copeland